under a gunmetal sky

under a gunmetal sky

101 short poems
20 longer poems

Larry Kimmel

café nietzsche press
windsor, ct

under a gunmetal sky

Published by
café nietzsche press
an imprint of:
bottle rockets press
p.o. box 189
windsor, ct 06095
www.bottlerocketspress.com
bottlerockets_99@yahoo.com

See also:

Winfred Press
364 Wilson Hill Road
Colrain, MA 01340
winfred@crocker.com
https://larry-kimmel.com/

Cover photo by Jasna Cuk
from Pixabay
Cover design by Larry Kimmel

ISBN: 979-8-9892491-4-5

Up above this world of care,
Han-Shan, old hand at solitaire.

<>

Author's Note

This collection is a sampler; that is, the poems are all to be found in other books of mine. I felt my *selected poems 1968 - 2022* was just too long, hence expensive, for many readers, but a book of 101 poems based on Japanese aesthetics with a section of 20 western-styled poems might be a more realistic way of reaching new readers and something more portable for old friends of my work.

under a gunmetal sky

Part 1

we did what we could

read their letters,
figured their taxes
good neighbors they

now just a cellar hole
and the lilacs in spring

with his coon cat coat
and feral green-eyed stare

Smoke, hale and hearty

we now speak of him
in the past tense
but keep the porchlight on

he was a dog
always with a project
he'd drop everything to say 'hello'
then back to his project – here,
the wild irises he transplanted

by lantern light
stacking pennies
five deep
& five deep –
waiting out the storm

at twilight the flame
in the bush is candlelight
caught by the window –
nothing more, nothing less
– is what you make of it

don't care much

for rasping dogmas
or chiseled tenets

my way
more like the wind
in the willows

that we can live on finer
& finer energy fields –
sure, why not?
if you can believe this world
you can believe any world

under a gunmetal sky
the goldenrod's strong yellow

mystique is where you make it so

a door
waits
to be opened

for fifty years
through all the weathers
of the mind,
I have loved the world with my eye
. . . if nothing else, that

you're gone

the rain rivulets down
our café window

how to say it?
Venus de Milo handcuffed
to a museum mind

urban midnight

in a pool of yellow lamplight
his craft or sullen art*

after long illness
an el Greco
in the garret window

midnight
a whistler and his footsteps

*Dylan Thomas – paraphrased

miles davis & blue lights

at this hour
some of the girls dance topless

at this hour
a spider slowly
yo-yos

Rorschach treescape
and moon fleeced clouds . . .
how unlikely,
against a yellow windowshade,
this perfect female profile

her skirt brightens
in the sunlight at the door
quick! quick!
her scissor shadow
cuts me through

selling flowers,
she wears
nothing but
the briefest briefs
beneath her dress

lovely to see,

but her snippy way
withers
my fine bouquet
of notions

in the night-fog
a yellow bruise
where the streetlight was –
any truth is better
than indefinite doubt

the tilt
of her head to undo
an earring –
fortresses crumble into
winter moonlight

I'm just saying
how good it is to see her
when suddenly
she sticks out her tongue –
catches a snowflake

having run out
of propane
we go to bed early –
her warmth the length of me
this winter night

on my back
on a bed
in a bed & breakfast –
my dime destiny
mapped on a cracked ceiling

after twenty years, again the room

the room my son
has rented unbeknownst

the room where I woke
to a carpet of spiders
that weren't

while I wait
to be served, I devise a story
in the willowware –
we've each of us our beliefs
and our own supporting evidence

biting the head off

the gingerbread man first,
I tell my 5 yr. old

that it's more humane
and
part of our oral tradition

Thanksgiving Day

candles and wine
a 3 lb. turkey

snow falling
through maple branches
a man and a woman . . .

at dusk

through sparse
& snow laden pines

boot tracks
enter
the woods

as I write

the kitten
rides
my wrist

winter
at the window

win, lose or checkmate
what difference?
my days of wine
and roses lost
in an unwritten book

my life
at the violet edge of day

no second draft

fears of
the dark walk
with me

in
the sugar bowl

the ants
are having the time
of their life

– let them

caught kissing

her dog
on the lips she laughs

pasture roses bloom
along the path
above the beach

putting out
kibble
for the feral cat
snow
on every branch

pigeons in a park

I feed them
and feed them

old humiliations
bob and coo
around me

the song writer
with little melody
before him

dreaming
of silent pianos

in dim & dusty rooms

in the light
of the hurricane lantern,
the walking stick
by the cabin door –
friend enough this winter night

November sunlight
slants
through the window

a chess board waits

with only
a few moves left

e x t e n d i n g his lifeline with a scalpel

crossing the churchyard in winter

on a headstone
her name yet not her name

the electric instant
before
I hurry on

a table set for two – a roast in the oven

the phone rings
in a white dress she goes out

whether by choice
or chance – she steps
into traffic

this past August,
all at once, the abuse of a decade
condensed into a bullet –
there's a house for sale
in our neighborhood

teasing the mirror, she strips

not wanting to waste
the few good years she sees

in the study below
her scholar husband
living a life of braille

she knew

but didn't know quite
why the many eyes caressed her

in a white skirt
with
the sun behind her

the restlessness of leaf shadows on a crimson couch

spring breezes open nightgowns

you leaned

against me
and neither of us

moved
for the longest
time

                    wearing
                    only
                    candlelight

                    my
                    buddy's
                    wife

this time, she tells me,

she's telling the truth –
between us

I watch the struggle
of a wasp drowning
in peach juice

cruel words
the inadequacy of long-stemmed roses

after seeing you off

taking the path along
the canal

a rustle of
leaves
underfoot

so that was that

now, breaking a dry stem
into bits

watching
the river
flow

midnight

you phone from another hemisphere
to say you're through with him –

a black widow
stands
on the ceiling

sunset after sunset

these solitary walks
this ache to tell

the fiery furnace
closes and leaves me
to my dusk

the door blows open

and the candles gutter
– the Ouija board

has just
spelt
d e a t h   h u r t s

will I outlive

this
economy size bottle

of vitamins?
that
is the question

all night with closed eyes

the ventriloquist's dummy lies
in its velvet box

for the first time
the muted many
dream their voices

lightning whitens the room,

naked
at the window

your afterimage
a ghostly
daguerreotype

silently in a snapshot

you are saying something
and look wonderful saying it

the fall leaves are gray
and your smile
is forever

where snowflakes become ocean
she takes my arm
                    the cry of gulls

shaking the stone from her shoe –
a white opal swings
        from between brown breasts

a dusting of snow
the chickadees's cluttered cuneiform

a dusting of snow

tramped
into lace
by tiny talons

the taste
of woodsmoke

in the black of night

in my mind's ear
the galloping thump of paw pads

the ghost
of a dog
sorely missed

"give it up, Tansy,

it's not going to fall off the limb
just because your canines are showing"

well,
the chipmunk
did fall

seeing you again

and so much of you
in your string bikini

evening's wild colors
flung
on sky and water

another scorcher

and the house
all to herself

a few
daring selfies –
why not ?

a cup
of
gossip

and you're gone

motes in a slant
of sunlight

after
one glass
of wine

the spill

of a decade's
discontent

the red
tinge

of tail lights
on
the snow

of your leaving

henge

under a blue sky
buttercups slope away to the sea

a long way from here
the headstone
awaiting me

granite

the
spacious

sound
of
nothing

on a sunlit rock

a passive pet
a corpse

the butterfly
whose wings in death are fixed
for flight

lifeless

from
the asphalt's
heat

and
swept aside
by traffic

thousands
of monarchs
litter

the roadside

the river,

all
trickle
&
bone

the leaves
pant

each grape
a raisin

apples float

and
muddy water clears

if
left
alone

in a gust of wind

a red leaf
hops
from the curb

I catch it

       at the sidewalk café
       some 3 or 4 sparrows
       gather at my feet –
       you have crumbs
       we have nooo crumbs

in Kate's Diner
under the plastic cake lid
– the necessary fly

she speaks of her past . . .
on her face the window prism's
iridescent bruise

working the grill

you should have seen his face
when the cops walked in

drugs
and underage videos
in an upstairs room

scandal, disaster,
rumors of war . . .

a fly

wrings its hands,
eats cake,
wrings its hands

icy roads
controlling the car with prayer & rectum

family in bed

and term papers graded
he steps, without hope,

into the snowy night
to see her
bedroom window lit

things believed to grant favors

angels, white witches
genies, relics
my upstairs tenant . . .

at the check-out,

her bewitching scent
woodsy-dark and pagan

some mother's son
tries to join
a coven

our fingers
touch

the small
arithmetic
of

coins

coffee
&
conversation

always
my back

to the wall

crabapple petals everywhere
I brush one
                from her cheek

she leaves in haste

she has to meet a *'friend'*
alone now,
I take up palette and brush

for that inexplicable
second caress

coal and steel
and the grit
that goes with them –
dandelion
was not a delicacy

first light

and again
I'm brewing coffee

like an ant
on a moebius strip
this dailiness

it nags, but

damn it, all I want
is to stand on the porch

and watch
the red leaves
fall

dusk
and the day lily all but done

the night is for the young
and for the solitaires
and I have been both –

soon, I will step into
the midnight forest,

become owl

the envelope
contained

a card, a photo,
a request for an autograph
and one

long blond hair

countless syllables

and still
and still

I've not
explained
myself

                    this creek

                    torrential in spring
                    a trickle now

                    all the things
                    in me
                    that wanted voice

as the water skier lets go
    slows &
                sinks, so
this epilogue
to a bookman's long career

where the small lake
leaks away . . .
    a tea-dark gurgle

      a dragonfly
      hovers

      then darts away

      you surface among
      the lily-pads
      wet and smiling

biting into an apple
warmed through by the sun

kicking a tin can

down
the
road

let the day lily
be
my metaphor

let
the long day end

just so

Part 2

I Step Out on My Porch Near Midnight

Snow,
flecked by moon made mica.

Cold, windless air—even
the roar of the woods
is faint tonight;

And faint, too,
the creak
of my leather jacket—faint

As the rigging of a galleon
heard across the seas of time . . .

While overhead
Orion faintly flickers.

The Wasp & The Spider

In the dust a wasp and spider caught
My boyish eye where they grappled and fought

Just when the spider broke free and ran
From the wasp that circled and circled again.

The spider's eight feet bought a foot
More desperate life for him till fate

Turned kamikaze and power dived down
On him. The sting was true! The brown

Back dimpled, doubled, rolled—a stricken
Ball of frenzied splinters, kicking.

The wasp backed away, became poised.
Arch-backed, wings spread, sure of her poison,

Gangly-legged now, her delicate toes
In the dust, she circled the stiffening throes.

The fight was done but I stayed stooped
Until the last leg slowed and stopped.

The Loft

There in the loft,
        where we had two mattresses
and between them
        a hurricane lantern,

I watched you sleep—saw
the grain of your hair flow
        dark
over the pillow and one white shoulder

laid bare by an errant quilt,
        a spill
of walnut over linen over almond;
        and heard

the wild wind ransacking
        the wastes of winter
in the edgeless black around us;
        heard it

rage around our parenthesis
of lantern light and love,
        our space capsule
between yesterday and tomorrow,

        our bubble (oblong) in a level,
I wished would never tilt.

October Elegy

After the burial she walked with me,
Where tall trees, standing in a clear
Sunlight, cast strict shadows across
The drive—a woman just past fifty,
Elegant and gracious, lovely to see.

"You came all the way from Maine, they say.
You must have been very fond of Kurt,"
Meaning her brother, my uncle by marriage,
and that was true.

A far hill seemed the reds and golds
Of an old tapestry kicked against
The horizon, while the branches near
At hand were clad in tatters, and one
Old oak in rags of penny-brown.

"You were just a boy when I left home."

That, too, was true, and true still,
The infatuation a boy once felt
For her—though now as mellow as
A bronze medallion smoothed by the wear
of a quarter century.

She took my arm, her white-gloved hand
Around my sleeve, and we walked awhile
In silence. Her step was steady, stately,
Despite the cant of her narrow heels
On the cinder drive. And leaving the drive
We crossed a quilt of yellow leaves,

Dimly reflected in the branches
Overhead, and I was made
Momentarily giddy by
the lightness of its color.

And as we joined the others, she let
Go of my arm, saying, "I must
See Joan before I leave," meaning
My aunt, her sister-in-law, and smiling
A smile of October charm she left me.

All that was eighteen years ago,
And now I am her age then, and now
I do not think that I shall ever
See her again, and that, I allow,
Is as it should be, now as the reds
And golds of old tapestry
Return, once more, to distant hills—
the same but not the same.

Of Destiny and Moonlight

In the moonlight the quilt has no color.
Is a patchwork of different darks, only.

In the woods the hoot owls are calling each
to each and my destiny is three score spent.

This afternoon you visited, wanting to talk
of old times. It seemed an adultery to comply.

Lying here, awake in the moonlight,
I recall an ingot of sunlight that lay

on the floor between us, a wrenched geometry
of gold that could not be lifted.

Lacuna

And in those days,
when living as if there were no tomorrow,

I woke not to a new day, but rather to the rewinding
of a watch. On the wall of the room where I slept

and changed clothes hung a three week calendar
that skipped to someday. Podunk and Now.

New Property

Scent of hot grasses. The sun a coin
of molten electrum. In a white dress

of thin muslin, her areolae bloom
dark as the plums warm from the tree.

With a thirst like this there's no help for it.
You thieve and wipe your chin,
laughing at the myth of ownership.

. . .

Wicked pretty
with eyes the blue
of burning alcohol,
eyes
to fuck a heart.

Woman Playing Guitar

Her breast
fit
like a fruit

in the curve
of the small guitar,

and I
would have been
her Picasso,

some
Spanish afternoon.

Waiting and Then Not Waiting for a Green Light In Greenfield, Massachusetts

The red pulse of three turn signals and the click
                                                    of my own
        —a serial music, more for the eye than the ear.

Images of unseen birds sweep the rear window
                                        of the car ahead,
like a school of neon tetras through an aquarium glass,
but swif' swift—each concise image pulled awry,
as the flock, itself, is warped, is bulged—is gone.

An hour ago: Gray whispery wisp of a man standing
a little less than the librarian on duty:
        " ... I have always been very sensitive,
very creative —yes-yes— have been all my life,
very sensitive, very creative ... " and on the street
outside the library, a drunk grabbed a parking meter,
stiffened—heaved
                                        —well there you have it,
a hot lunch.   And now it is—the awaited shift from red
to green—the tachometer needle jumps.
                                        (When you redline
on fear you redline, and everybody has a battlefield,
and it doesn't matter where or what the battlefield
when you redline).
                        I still have 20 minutes on a meter
in Brattleboro—but that's another town, another state.

"REDLINE MY HEART 3-PERSONED GOD!" I'm coming
                home, home to meat and potatoes
                                        and look at that!—

92

old apple tree? or bonsai and me incredibly shrunk?

All these years, I have been wasting, wasting,
                                    wasting the poem.

The Class Ring

I hold in my hand a ring. Moxium High.
Class of '58. The initials my own.
Within weeks, I'd left it by a public sink.
Loss noted and steps retraced—both

immediate, but ... *c'est la vie*. Seven
years later it returned, having found
its way to the alma mater with its
postal pedigree, some half-dozen

other Moxiums. A worthy scholarship,
the particulars of that seven year odyssey,
which remains mute within the zero of
this prodigal trinket of youth, inanimate

wanderer, whose encircled secret rests
upon my palm, yet forever beyond my grasp.

Spring Woods

Skunk-cabbages that yesterday were green
napkins folded to stand upright, now forge
the bog, swarm the wooded hillside . . .

        across the path
        a snake
        too cold to care

Strange Harvest

His first day home on the farm, unscathed by combat, he loses a leg to the harvester.

last night
a sister's auburn hair
this morning white

Bright Days

_____

Bright days, hand-in-hand—what a friendship we had then! You said, "The river is shampooing its hair," and we played Pooh sticks from its bridge.

       that glint
          in the forest –
              where did it go?

_____

Herr Stein

———————————————

I can still hear Herr Stein saying: " ... but it is a good
F, in fact, if there was such a thing as an F+, that's
what it would be."

> at the nursing home
> explaining myself
> to a puzzled man . . .

———————————————

The Doe

_____

As the headlights touch her, her legs fold to unfold on
the far side of the fence where she isn't . . . having
vanished into thin dusk . . .

gone -
but the wonder
of blood and spirit
remains

_____

From Now On

She sleeps beside me bathed in moonlight. Saw what I saw, know what I know. Great sex still, but no heart for lovemaking.

> is this it?
> an empty canoe
> on a river
> slow
> as from now on

Another Take on Saturday Morning

_____

Would like to be dark-haired, handsome, lean as a hickory, famous, and have a sense of well being—all on the same day.

    greying at the temple
    and still "the poem"
    unwritten

_____

New England Palms

Somewhere between weed and tree, the sumacs that jungle my unkempt property. I like them. My neighbors don't. I call them New England palms.

cliffside cottage
blue hills in the distance
here I could be
a Ryōkan
or a Han Shan

Seeking The Hermit-Sage

I see myself on a mountain, an old man
loafing in sunlight, who long since came seeking
the hermit-sage, who not finding him,
lingered, among the pines, a night, a day,

another night and day, to this very hour.
Loafing, I finger the beads of incidents past:
recall the earth-cave found beneath an oak;
the foraged-food enough; and the learned-fire,

friend against winter; the rude hut built;
and the quieting of mind, which I compare
to the slow clearing of muddied water. And now,
on this ledge, as an old man reflecting, loafing

in sun-warmth, it simply comes to me that I
am he, found at last—the hermit-sage.

Branch after Branch

Slats of clear gold sunlight
and snow like fur on every branch
and every branch after branch after branch
as far as thought can reach . . .

I go to see if our road's been plowed.
The many small birds melt
before my boots and frosty breath.

Branch after branch, vast in its snowy hush,
the universe is as big as you think it is—

and maybe one or two trees more.

Acknowledgment is made to the following magazine and book publications where some of these poems first appeared: American Tanka; Atlas Poetica; Bamboo Hut; bedtime story, gembun anthology 9, empty press; Blue Smoke; bottle rockets; Bright Stars; chaba (e-zine); Colrain Clarion; Concise Delight; dew-on-line; Erotic Haiku, editied by Hiroaki Sato; Eucalypt; Fire Pearls; frogpond; Haiku 21.2, an anthology by Modern Haiku Press; Haiku Headlines; HSA Member's Anthology, 1997; Hummingbird; Ink, Sweat & Tears; its own place (anthology) 2018; light-borne rain; Lights Across the River; LYNX; Magnapoets; Modern English Tanka; Modern Haiku; MOONGARLIC; Morning Song, St. Martin's Press; NeverEnding Story; Poetry in the Light; Poetry Today; RAW NerVZ Haiku; Ribbons; still, a journal of short verse; Skylark; Simply Haiku; Tanka Café; Tanka Splendor; The Christian Science Monitor; the cherita; The Green Age Literary Review; The Japan Times; The Tanka Journal; TSA Newsletter; TSA members" anthology; This Wood Sang Out, an anthology; Woodnotes; World Haiku Review – poetry bridge.

Other Books of Poetry by Larry Kimmel

in an upstairs room

this hunger, tissue-thin

outer edges

the colors of ash

the horizon waits

Adrift

diminishing into mist

thunder and apple blossoms:
selected haiku

Collected Haiku: 1997 – 2017

selected poems 1968 - 2022

a river years from here

Unworldly Wind

Second Chance & other tales ...
(novella & short stories of Whip-poor-will Hollow)